LIVING
FOSSILS

Written by
Joyce Pope

Illustrated by
Stella Stilwell and Helen Ward

STECK-VAUGHN
L I B R A R Y
A Division of Steck-Vaughn Company

Austin, Texas

Editor: Andy Charman
Designer: Mike Jolley
Picture research: Jenny Faithful

Library of Congress Cataloging-in-Publication Data

Pope, Joyce.
Living fossils / written by Joyce Pope : illustrated by Stella Stillwell
and Helen Ward.
p. cm. – (Curious creatures)
Includes index.
Summary: Examines living animals and plants that have managed to survive
as species over millions of years without undergoing change, including the
shark, crocodile, horseshoe crab, and magnolia.
ISBN 0-8114-3151-7
1. Living fossils – Juvenile literature. [1. Living fossils.]
I. Stillwell, Stella, ill. II. Ward, Helen, 1962- ill. III. Title. IV. Series.
QL88.5.P66   1991   91-13998
574–dc20   CIP AC

NOTES TO READER
There are some words in this book that are printed in **bold** type.
A brief explanation of these words is given in the glossary on p. 45.

All living things are given a Latin name when first classified by a scientist.
Some of them also have a common name. For example, the common name
of *Sturnus vulgaris* is common starling. In this book we use other Latin words,
such as larva and pupa. We make these words plural by adding an "e",
for example, one larva becomes many larvae (pronounced lar-vee).

Color separations by Positive Colour Ltd., Maldon, Essex, Great Britain
Printed and bound by L.E.G.O., Vicenza, Italy

1 2 3 4 5 6 7 8 9 0 LE 96 95 94 93 92

CONTENTS

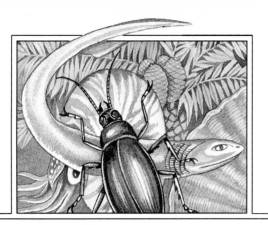

FORGOTTEN BY TIME

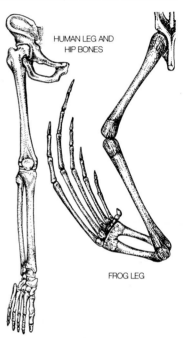

▼ Below, you can see the leg bones of a human being and a frog. You can see that one basic design has been used to make the support for two very different kinds of legs. It is possible to find likenesses of this kind in both living and fossil creatures. The bodies of fishes, frogs, lizards, dinosaurs, birds, and mammals are all built on a similar pattern. Without exception, they have a flexible row of backbones between the head and the tail. Because of this, scientists group them together as the **vertebrates**, or backboned animals.

HUMAN LEG AND HIP BONES

FROG LEG

The phrase "living fossils" sounds like nonsense, because we usually think of a fossil as a dead thing. Most plant and animal **species** die out after a few million years of existence. "Living fossils" is the term often used to describe a small number of creatures that seem to be caught in a time warp. Bypassed by events around them, they have not died out and have not changed over many millions of years.

There are many reasons why living fossils have survived unchanged. Sometimes it is because the **environment** in which they live has not altered and so they have not been forced to adapt. Often, a species dies out because it is replaced by another one which is more successful. This new species may be a more efficient hunter or better at escaping from **predators**. Many living fossils have survived because they live in isolated places away from competition with other kinds of life. Others survive because they are already the best at what they do.

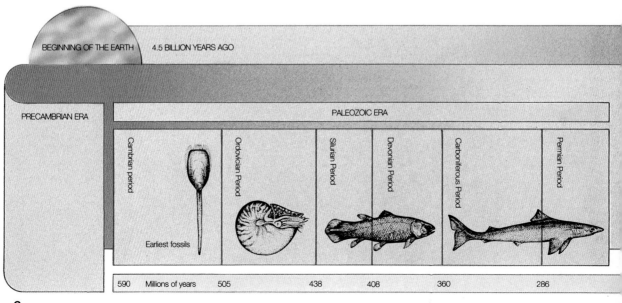

BEGINNING OF THE EARTH | 4.5 BILLION YEARS AGO

PRECAMBRIAN ERA

PALEOZOIC ERA

Cambrian period

Earliest fossils

Ordovician Period

Silurian Period

Devonian Period

Carboniferous Period

Permian Period

| 590 | Millions of years | 505 | 438 | 408 | 360 | 286 |

Takahe

The takahe is a large, flightless bird. It was thought to be **extinct**, but in 1948 a small number were found alive in the Murchison Mountains of South Island, New Zealand. Not many survived, possibly due to changes in climate. Human activities have made it even more difficult for these birds to survive. Weasels, brought from Europe, killed the chicks, and red deer competed with the birds for their food. The takahe is now preserved in the Fiordland National Park, New Zealand, and the population may number as many as 250. Studies of living takahes tell us many things that their bones alone could not. For example, takahes use their feet to hold down food. They also mate for life. In this way living fossils help us to understand better the true fossil bones dug up from the rocks.

Measuring Time

Fossils tell us that there has been abundant life on earth for at least 600 million years. That time is divided into three great eras. These are the Paleozoic, Mesozoic, and the Cenozoic eras, as you can see from the chart on the left. They are separated from each other by great changes in the kinds of fossils found. Each era is divided into periods, based on lesser changes in fossils. The names of the periods are usually taken from the places where rocks of that age were first discovered.

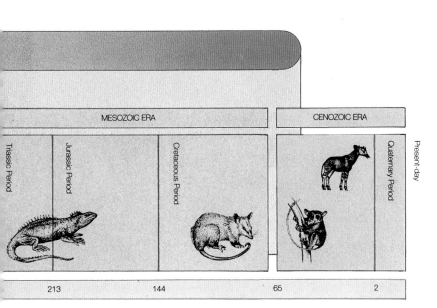

MESOZOIC ERA

CENOZOIC ERA

Triassic Period

Jurassic Period

Cretaceous Period

Quaternary Period

Present-day

213   144   65   2

FISHES

Most of the fishes alive today belong to a group that has been on earth for about 100 million years. Only a few kinds have survived from earlier times. Sturgeons and gar pikes, for example, are armored with bone or heavy scales, like many ancient fishes. The most famous of all living fossil fishes is the coelacanth.

COELACANTHS

Scientists have studied fossil coelacanths for the past 100 years. The oldest of these fossil fishes dates back about 400 million years. Coelacanths are interesting because they are similar to the fishes that first took to life on land. One of the most important parts of the research is to try to discover the relationship between coelacanths and these early fishes.

Coelacanth Circus Act
Living coelacanths have been observed head downward near the sea bed. They are probably hunting, using a special ability to detect tiny electric currents given off by the muscles of little fishes and shrimps.

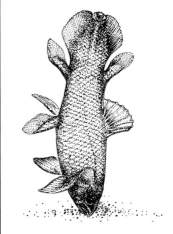

▼ These present-day coelacanths live in cold, deep water, where they feed on small fishes and cuttlefishes. When swimming slowly, they balance with the fins on their backs and use their other fins as though they were walking through the water. Coelacanths can shoot forward faster with a swish of their tails.

Just before Christmas in 1938 a strange fish was caught off the coast of South Africa and was taken to the local museum. Unfortunately it could not be completely preserved but enough survived for the remains to be recognized as those of a coelacanth. Professor J.L.B. Smith studied the fish and 14 years later found another near the Comoro Islands near Madagascar. Others have since been caught in this area.

A number of coelacanths have been studied in laboratories where it has been found that most of the skeleton is made of gristlelike **cartilage**. The heart is simpler in shape than that of any other fish and the brain is tiny. Coelacanths grow to a length of 5 feet, which is larger than any of their fossil ancestors.

Since their discovery, over 100 coelacanths have been caught. It is certain that very few remain alive. Without strict **conservation**, these last survivors of ancient times will soon become extinct.

▼ This coelacanth is a preserved specimen from a museum. Coelacanths once lived in many **habitats**, but are now found only in deep water. They have probably survived because their environment has remained unchanged and because they live in relative isolation from other kinds of life.

SHARKS

Fossil hunters found the first remains of sharks in rocks that are about 380 million years old. As a rule, only the teeth were fossilized because they were the only hard parts of the body. Then, as now, sharks had skeletons made of tough cartilage rather than bone and this very rarely formed fossils.

The fishes that lived at the same time as these early sharks have become extinct leaving few descendants. Though the sharks themselves have changed in detail, the group as a whole has survived. Like their ancestors, most sharks are streamlined, fast-swimming hunters living in the upper waters of warm seas. Sharks are the largest of all fishes. The very biggest are **filter feeders**, but even the active hunters are larger than the biggest bony fishes, such as barracuda.

Many kinds of sharks have become rare because they have been overfished by humans. Once numbers are low, it is difficult for them to recover quickly. This is because sharks breed slowly. They either lay a small number of large, yolky eggs or produce living young.

Living sharks can teach us more than extinct ones. Very few diseases are known in sharks. Even cancer, which has been discovered in most other kinds of animals, is practically unknown among them. Perhaps the study of sharks could help us conquer cancer.

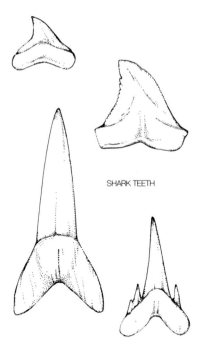

SHARK TEETH

▲ Sharks have large numbers of teeth. When one becomes worn or broken, it falls out and is replaced by another that grows up behind it. The teeth of most fossil sharks are very similar to those of living species, telling us that their food and their way of hunting have not changed through the ages. Some fossil sharks had teeth that are much larger than the teeth of present-day sharks.

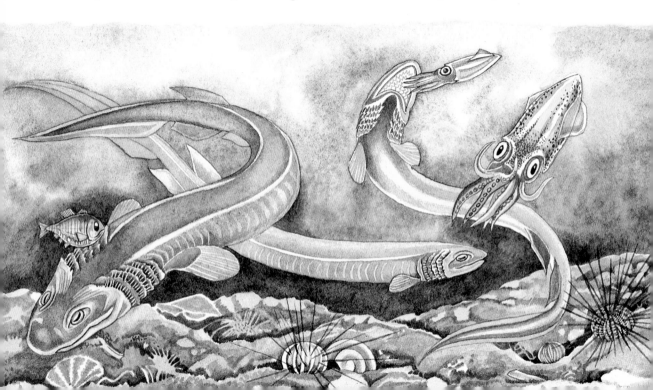

Living Fossil Shark

Below, you can see the jaw of a Port Jackson shark. This species of shark lives in shallow seas, mainly off the coast of South Australia. It has some sharp pointed teeth in the front of its mouth, but the teeth at the back of its jaws are broad and ridged. They are used for crushing the hard shells of crabs, sea urchins, and oysterlike creatures that are its only food. Fossil teeth of exactly the same kind have been found in rocks in Europe, dating back over 150 million years. They were known before the living fish was discovered.

JAW OF PORT JACKSON SHARK

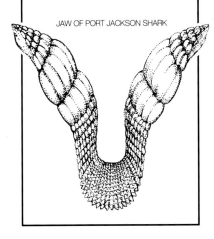

▲ This sand tiger shark has razor-sharp teeth. The teeth point inward. This makes it hard for the shark's **prey** to escape once it has been caught.

◀ Six-gilled sharks like these relatives of today's frilled shark are mostly extinct. The frilled shark is a living fossil that survives in deep, cold water. Its number of gill slits and the way that its jaw is attached to its skull make it seem like many kinds of sharks of the past.

11

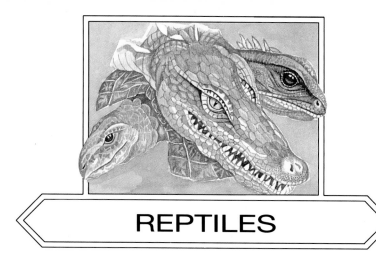

REPTILES

The great days of the prehistoric **reptiles** – the dinosaurs, the flying reptiles, and the sea monsters – are over. The crocodiles, turtles, and tuatara that survive to the present day had ancestors that were alive at the same time as the dinosaurs. They have changed very little over the centuries.

CROCODILES

Crocodiles are closely related to dinosaurs. This can be seen in many ways. Their bones show us that they have the same skull structure and their teeth grow in a similar way. Like almost all dinosaurs, crocodiles have much bigger hind legs than front legs and are protected by bony armor.

Dinosaurs were mainly land-living creatures, but

Armed to the Teeth
True crocodiles have a notch on either side of the upper jaw. The fourth tooth in the lower jaw slots into this and can be seen when the mouth is closed.

Alligators and caimans have short, rather blunt jaws. Their large lower teeth fit into pits and cannot be seen when the mouth is closed.

The gharial has very long jaws with fine teeth for catching fish.

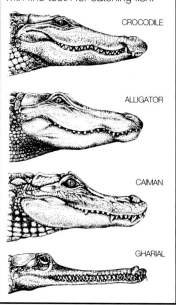

CROCODILE

ALLIGATOR

CAIMAN

GHARIAL

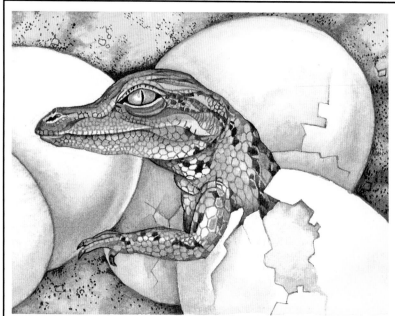

Hatching Out
All living crocodiles hatch from eggs, which are usually laid in a nest close to the water. The female stays nearby. When she hears squeaks from inside the eggs, she uncovers them and in some cases carries the babies to the water in her mouth.

The earliest crocodiles probably behaved in a similar way although their nests have not been found. Recently, the sites of breeding colonies of dinosaurs have been found. In some, the offspring left the nest soon after hatching. Others remained in the nest and were cared for by their parents.

crocodiles took to the water, which is where we still find them. They swim using their large flattened tails, but often float gently up to their prey, with only their nostrils above the water. A crocodile is able to grab and hold a struggling animal under water because, as it breathes, air flows into a separate channel above its mouth and into its throat. This channel can be closed with a flap of skin, so that no water is swallowed, or gets into the lungs.

Today, most crocodiles and their relatives live beside rivers or lakes. Only the estuarine crocodile is regularly found in the sea. In the Jurassic Period, however, many crocodiles lived in the sea. Their feet were paddlelike, and their tails ended in a fishlike fin. They must have been expert sea-hunters. They had long **snouts** and strong, sharp teeth. One fossil has stomach stones stained black with the ink of fast-swimming squidlike creatures on which it fed.

▼ The largest living crocodile measures about 25 feet long. In the past, some, such as *Phobosuchus* (shown below), were twice this size. These monsters probably ambushed dinosaurs as they came to the river to drink.

There are also dwarves among the earliest crocodiles. Some were no more than 19 inches long when fully grown. They probably fed on insects and some of the tiny early mammals that lived at the same time as the dinosaurs.

TURTLES AND TORTOISES

Tortoises are often kept as pets and so they seem ordinary to us. Yet they are living fossils, descendants of animals that existed before the first dinosaurs.

Turtles, terrapins, and tortoises belong to a group of over 200 reptiles known scientifically as the Chelonia. These creatures are encased in an armor made of bone and horn, and their lives are controlled by this shell. Even breathing and mating are difficult. They are living proof that success and survival need not depend on being able to move quickly.

Living chelonians have no teeth. Instead, they cut their food with sharp, horny beaks. Tortoises feed on plants; terrapins are flesh eaters. Marine turtles eat many sorts of food. The leathery turtle is the largest of these. It feeds on jellyfishes.

Although they have survived for so long, the large chelonians are all **endangered**, mainly through human activity. The biggest land tortoises now survive in tiny numbers on remote islands and the egg-laying sites of sea turtles are under threat for many reasons.

BOWSPRIT TORTOISE

DIAMONDBACK TERRAPIN

GREEN TURTLE

Living in a Shell
Tortoises have heavy, domed shells and short, stubby feet. Terrapins, which spend most of their time in water, have flatter, lighter shells and many have webbed feet, which help them to swim. Marine turtles are all large with fairly light shells and big flippers for swimming.

▶ *Archelon* was an ancestor of the present-day turtles. It was a big sea-living turtle. It lived about 80 million years ago in warm seas that covered land which is now part of Europe and America.

◀ This green turtle's shell has two sections. The **carapace** covers the back and the **plastron** protects the underparts. Land, and most freshwater, species can pull their heads, tails, and legs under cover so that they are safe from almost all attackers. The shell is also a disadvantage because it is attached to the animal's vertebrae, ribs, hips, and shoulders. This restricts the animal's breathing, which is by pumping movements of the throat. Box turtles, shown below, have hinged shells that can be completely closed around them.

SKULL OF *TRIASSOCHELYS* SHOWING ROOF OF MOUTH

TRIASSOCHELYS

Toothed Turtles

Triassochelys, which lived more than 200 million years ago, is one of the earliest chelonians known. Its shell was like that of present-day chelonians – it was made of bone, covered with plates of finger-naillike horn. An important difference was in its jaws, because the roof of its mouth was studded with small teeth. Some descendants of *Triassochelys* were among the largest and strangest of all chelonians. One, which lived in Australia less than a million years ago, had horns on its head. Its head was more than 18 inches across.

TUATARAS

Tuataras look like heavily-built lizards, but they are in fact living fossils that have scarcely changed for 200 million years. They survived for many centuries in New Zealand, where the ancient Maoris gave them their odd name, which means "spiny back." They now live only on a few small islands near the coast of New Zealand's North Island. They eat mainly insects, although they also eat snails and earthworms.

Tuataras' whole lives seem to be organized on a slow clock. Resting tuataras may not need to breathe more than once an hour. Not surprisingly, they grow slowly but live a long time. Male tuataras may be over 2 feet long, and weigh over 2 pounds, and live to be more than 100 years of age. This slowness starts in the eggs. These are laid in the early summer, in a hole dug by the female.

New Zealand

NORTH ISLAND

COOK STRAIT

TASMAN SEA

PACIFIC OCEAN

SOUTH ISLAND

▲ The tuatara probably became extinct on mainland New Zealand because it was preyed upon by rats, cats, and pigs introduced by the English. It is now confined to small islands where these predators do not exist.

▼ The tuatara is the only survivor of a group of reptiles that lived 250 to 70 million years ago. This group is known as "the beak-heads." *Paradepedon huxleyi*, shown below, was a distant cousin of the tuatara. It was 6 feet long and had a powerful beak which it used to crush roots.

◄ In its remote home, this tuatara has no natural enemies. This remoteness is the main reason why tuataras have survived for so long. Unlike most lizards, they do not need to be agile fast-moving creatures.

Each egg is about 3 inches long, and has a leathery shell of a brownish-pink color. It takes more than a year for the baby tuataras to hatch.

Tuataras look like lizards and are like them in many ways. For instance, if a tuatara breaks its tail, a new one will grow. Also, the tuatara has a sort of eye, the pineal eye, set in the top of its head. It doesn't look like an eye, but light can get through a special scale to a **lens** and light-sensitive cells below. This pineal eye is highly developed in adult tuataras. Nobody knows what the pineal eye is for, but some people think that it may help the lizards to control body temperature and the ability to be active in cool weather.

▲ The tuatara has a crest of large spines along its neck, back, and tail. In the male, these spines become erect when it is excited or hunting.

Sharing a Burrow

Tuataras live in burrows, and only come out at night to feed. They prefer cool, damp nights because they can be active at much lower temperatures than any other species of reptile.

Tuataras either dig their own burrows or share one with a petrel (a kind of seabird). They can only live on islands where the topsoil has been loosened by the burrowing of these birds. The lizards and the birds do not always live happily together. The tuataras often eat the petrels' eggs or chicks and occasionally even adult birds.

MAMMALS

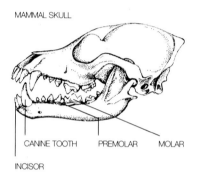

▼ Below you can see the skull of a mammal. Mammals have several different types of teeth in their jaws. In the front are single-rooted teeth for nipping, called incisors. At each corner of the jaws is a large, pointed tooth called the canine tooth. Behind these are larger teeth with several roots. They are called the premolar and molar teeth. They are used for chewing or grinding food. Teeth are the parts of an animal most likely to become fossilized.

MAMMAL SKULL

CANINE TOOTH PREMOLAR MOLAR

INCISOR

We can tell that a fossil is that of a mammal from its teeth and the shape of its bones. We cannot say whether the earliest creatures with mammallike bones were warm blooded, furry, and fed their young on milk like all modern mammals, but we assume that this was the case. The majority of mammals alive today have fossil relatives. It is not surprising that this should be so, for many fossil mammals date back only a few thousands or millions of years as you can see from the chart on pages 6 and 7. A small number of mammals, however, have survived almost unchanged since the last days of the dinosaurs. They give us an idea of what the first mammals may have been like.

Open Wide
A yawning opossum shows its teeth. These are small and sharp, suitable for eating insects and small creatures such as lizards or baby mice. Some opossums also eat fruit. Teeth are the hardest part of an animal's body. For this reason, the teeth of small animals often become fossilized, but the more fragile bones are destroyed. The teeth of early fossil opossums are very similar to those of present-day opossums. This shows that they fed on the same kinds of food.

OPOSSUMS

Small, pouched mammals called opossums have lived in the forests of South America for about 60 million years. Fossil teeth, similar to those of living opossums have been found in many parts of South America. It is probable that some of these early animals traveled from South America to Antarctica. From Antarctica, they traveled into Australia before the continents split into their present form. In Australia, these early mammals developed into the many different kinds of pouched mammals that are found there today.

The mouse opossums are the smallest of the group. These little creatures are mostly active at night. They are wary, agile creatures. During the daytime they shelter in nests made of leaves and twigs. It is likely that early mammals lived in a similar way.

▼ Most present-day opossums have long, hairless tails, which are sometimes covered with scaly skin. Small, climbing opossums, like the one shown here, have a **prehensile tail**, used as a fifth hand. In some cases the animal can even swing from it. We do not know exactly what the tails of early opossums were like, but they may also have had prehensile tails.

◄ Opossum babies are about the size of a grain of rice when they are born. They crawl to their mother's **pouch** where they are protected and fed for about two months. After this they ride on her back when she goes out to hunt at night. Early opossums probably behaved in the same way.

TARSIERS

Tarsiers are rarely seen, because they are active only at night. You would have to travel to Celebes or some of the other islands around the coast of southeast Asia to find them in the wild. In the past, similar creatures lived in North America and Europe. Tarsiers have survived with very little change for about 45 million years.

The best preserved fossils of early tarsiers are of skulls and teeth. These give us an idea of the general size, the type of food they ate, and tells us a little about how the animals lived. We can draw a reasonable picture of an extinct animal from this evidence.

Modern tarsiers get their name because their foot, or tarsal, bones are very long. Long tarsal bones enable them to jump about in the branches as they hunt for the insects and other small creatures that are their food. A tarsier, which has a head and body length of about 6 inches and weighs about 15 ounces, can jump about 6 feet. In order to do this, it must be able to judge distances very well. This is possible because a tarsier's eyes look forward. Animals like rabbits whose eyes are on the sides of their heads are able to see behind them but they cannot judge distances in front.

The tarsier is **nocturnal** and comes out to feed at night. Its huge eyes gather light in the darkness, allowing the tarsier to be a good nighttime hunter.

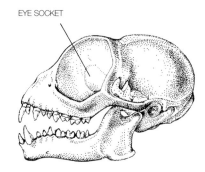

EYE SOCKET

▲ This picture of a tarsier's skull shows how its huge eyes take up most of the front of its face. Its jaws and sharp, pointed teeth look tiny. The tarsier's brain is much larger than that of most other small animals. The size of the tarsier's brain and the shape of its face bones show us that it is related to monkeys and apes.

◀ The tarsier's huge eyes and ears tell us that its sight and hearing are very good. Its sense of smell is poor. It uses its long tail to balance itself when it jumps. Tarsiers seem to live alone or in pairs, but these are part of larger groups, which keep in touch mainly by sound and scent. Tarsiers may have survived for so long because they live on islands and are isolated from competition with other kinds of life.

▼ Great tropical forests, like the one shown below, once spread across much of the land that now forms North America and Europe. About 50 million years ago they were the home of animals much like the tarsiers of today. The creatures that shared this home were very different from anything alive at present. They included the earliest ancestors of horses and rhinoceroses.

Tarsiers are especially important to **paleontologists** because they are blueprint creatures. Their forward-pointing eyes and short jaws are like those of present-day monkeys and apes. We think that the ancestors of these animals were very much like tarsiers. From fossil clues we know that early tarsiers had smaller eyes than present-day tarsiers. One thing that we do not know about the early tarsiers is whether they could turn their heads in almost a complete circle as the modern ones can.

Like many animals of tropical forests, tarsiers are threatened by the destruction of their habitat.

▼ Below, you can see in detail what a tarsier's foot looks like. The end part of each toe (and each finger) is flattened, and covered with wrinkled skin, like very deep fingerprints. These toes act like suction pads, and enable the animal to grip onto smooth surfaces. In captivity it can even leap and hold onto a vertical sheet of glass. Two toes on each foot have claws instead of nails. The tarsier uses these for grooming its fur.

TARSIER FOOT

CLAWS

TARSIER HAND

Getting a Grip

A tarsier's safety in the forest depends largely on its hands and feet. It can grasp small branches and hold on very tightly. The tarsier is able to do this because the thumb and the big toe can be folded across the palm of the hand or sole of the foot. We can do this with our thumbs but not our toes; it is known as having an **opposable** toe. The tarsier has flat nails on the tips of its fingers.

MOUNTAIN BEAVERS

The mountain beaver is poorly named. It is a **rodent**, but not a beaver. It does not live in high mountains though it is always found by water. A mountain beaver lives in a maze of tunnels that lead from its nest of dry leaves to a nearby stream. It feeds entirely on green vegetation and stores twigs and leaves for the winter.

Its small brain and the way in which its jaws work are clues that the mountain beaver is related to the earliest of all rodents.

◀ The mountain beaver is related to the earliest of all rodents that lived from about 60 million to 30 million years ago. It is found only in western North America, though its ancestors lived in Europe and Asia as well. There are now more kinds of rodents or gnawing animals than any other kinds of mammals.

Paramys, pictured below, was one of the first rodents. It looked like a squirrel, but its skeleton was like that of the mountain beaver.

OKAPIS

The okapi was one of the last large animals to be discovered by scientists. Fossils of giraffelike creatures similar to it were discovered in Asia in the 1860s, but these had been extinct for over 5 million years.

The first clue to the existence of the okapi was a note in an explorer's account of the Congo forests. He said that the pygmies hunted a creature that they described as a donkey, though he did not see one. In 1899, the governor of Uganda asked a group of pigmies about this creature and was told that it was like a striped mule that was often killed for food. He managed to get part of the striped skin and thought that it must be a zebra of some kind. Later he was sent a whole skin and a skull. Then he realized that, in spite of the stripes, the animal was a short-necked giraffe.

The okapi is active during the daytime, but it is not often seen. This is because it usually lives alone and is very wary. Its sense of hearing is excellent and it flees from the least sound that might mean danger. It feeds on the leaves and fruit of many kinds of forest plants.

Okapis have survived because they are isolated in their dense forest home. As long as this forest home survives, they are probably safe from extinction.

▶ Okapis, like the one shown here, are kept in many zoos. They survive well in captivity and have reached ages of up to 33 years. Most okapis in zoos today have been bred there. One female produced 12 calves, the last when she was 26 years old. The animals may be transported long distances to suitable mates.

SIVATHERIUM

▲ *Sivatherium* was a relative of the giraffe and okapi of today, though it did not look like either of them. Its body was about the same size and shape as an elk and it had very large antlers. It probably lived in the same sort of way as big deer of the present day. It did not become extinct until after humans arrived in India and North Africa. They made drawings and statuettes of an animal that archeologists think is meant to be *Sivatherium*.

◀ *Giraffokeryx* was an ancestor of the okapis we see today. You can see by comparing this picture with the photograph of the present-day okapi that okapis have not changed very much over time.

Reaching Out

Giraffes and okapis look quite different, but they belong to the same family. One of the things they have in common is a long tongue. A giraffe can stick its tongue out over 18 inches. An okapi has a tongue so long that the animal can use it to clean its eyes. Long tongues help the animals to gather food. The tongue is very strong and flexible. It is wrapped around small twigs and a mouthful of leaves is stripped off. We do not know about the tongues of early okapis. The fossils that we find are, however, so similar to living members of the family in so many other ways that it is likely that they also had long tongues.

GIRAFFE

OKAPI

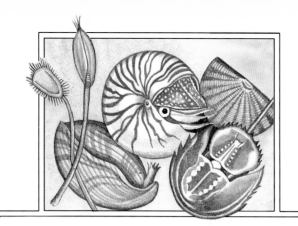

SEA CREATURES

Most of the fossils we find are the remains of sea creatures. In the oceans of today we find survivors of many ancient groups of animals. They are usually rare. Some have not changed since the Paleozoic Era.

LAMP SHELLS

You are more likely to find a fossil lamp shell than a living one. More than 30,000 extinct kinds are known, but today only about 300 species exist. Some of these are rarely seen, because they live in deep, cold water. Others may live in sandy places or are attached to rocks, but generally people pass by them, thinking that they

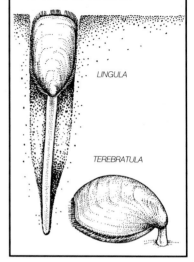

Lamp Shells

Lingula, which has an oval, horny shell, lives in a burrow in the sand. *Terebratula* attaches itself to rock. Some spiny fossil types lived on sandy surfaces.

LINGULA

TEREBRATULA

▼ These fossil lamp shells from Ohio are over 350 million years old. When they were alive they were among the most common animals in the sea. Since then, lamp shells have gradually been replaced by other kinds of animals.

are clams. This is because lamp shells, like clams, mussels, and scallops, are formed in two parts. Unlike clams, however, lamp shells always have one shell that is bigger than the other and where they join there is a small, round hole. A fleshy stalk comes through this hole and attaches the shell to the rock or sea bed.

Lamp shells take water into their shells and remove from it tiny scraps of food. They also take oxygen that they need. This way of living uses up little energy because it uses the same action for two important functions. Some lamp shell species have survived in this way, without change, for over 500 million years.

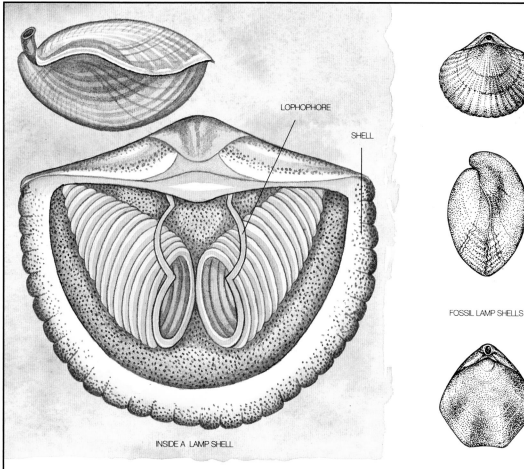

LOPHOPHORE

SHELL

FOSSIL LAMP SHELLS

INSIDE A LAMP SHELL

The "Arm-foot" Shell

Above is a diagram that shows how a lamp shell is formed. To the right are some examples of fossil lamp shells with differently shaped shells. The scientific name for lamp shells is "brachiopods."

Brachiopod means "arm-foot." Inside the shell, is the **lophophore**.

This is an arm or ribbon of limy or horny material that loops from one side of the shell to the other.

People once thought that the lamp shell used the lophophore for moving about, which is how it got its name. In fact, the lophophore supports a large number of small tentacles. When the shells are

open, these tentacles move, making currents that circulate water. Oxygen is taken in through the thin skin of the tentacles, and food particles are swept toward the mouth. Before the water is pushed out of the shell, carbon dioxide and other waste materials are added to it.

CHAMBERED NAUTILUSES

Over 3,000 species of fossil nautiluses are known. They once lived in all the seas of the world. Today, only six kinds survive in the southwest Pacific Ocean. The earliest relative of the chambered nautilus lived about 500 million years ago. It had a straight shell, like a chimney. Later nautiluses developed shells that were coiled in a flat spiral. Present-day kinds are this shape.

The chambered nautilus belongs to a group of animals that includes octopuses, cuttlefish, and squids. Their scientific name is cephalopod, which means "head-foot." The cephalopods move by jet propulsion, forcing water through a tube just below their heads. Like its relatives, the chambered nautilus is a flesh eater, tearing its food with a heavy parrotlike beak. Unlike them, it does not have a poisonous bite. It has about 90 tentacles on its head. They are not covered with suckers like those of the octopus, but with a sticky material, which helps the nautilus to hold its food.

▶ Nautiluses, like the one shown here, are rarely seen swimming in open water. They usually stay on or near the sea bottom, at a depth of about 1,200 feet. They swim slowly as they feed along the edge of a reef. Their main food is crabs and shrimp, which they probably find by using their sense of smell. Males, which may have shells as much as 10 inches across, are slightly larger than females. Nautiluses seem to breed slowly. The females produce only about 10 large eggs in a year. Most other cephalopods lay thousands of eggs.

▼ These are ancient relatives of today's chambered nautilus. It is not possible to tell from fossils exactly what color they were, but they show patterns of stripes and zigzags. These patterns may have helped to camouflage the nautiluses.

Weightless in Water

A chambered nautilus weighs about 3 pounds in air but less than an ounce in water. This is because it carries gas. This is trapped in the 30 or more chambers into which its shell is divided. New chambers are formed as the animal grows. To begin with, the last empty chamber fills with water. This water is gradually removed by a tube, called the **siphuncle**. This runs through the shell from the last wall, or **septum**, to the first and smallest living space. It takes at least a month to empty a chamber and replace the liquid with air from which most of the oxygen has been removed. The working of the siphuncle is complex as it has to overcome the force of water pressure at great depths.

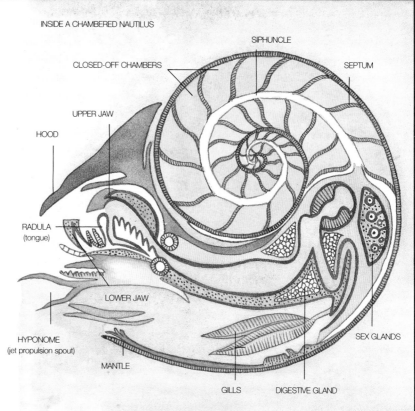

INSIDE A CHAMBERED NAUTILUS

SIPHUNCLE

SEPTUM

CLOSED-OFF CHAMBERS

UPPER JAW

HOOD

RADULA
(tongue)

LOWER JAW

HYPONOME
(jet propulsion spout)

MANTLE

GILLS

DIGESTIVE GLAND

SEX GLANDS

The nautilus is the only living cephalopod with an extended shell. The shell is divided into a series of chambers, in the last and largest of which the animal lives. When it is threatened, it can close the opening with a tough, leatherlike hood.

Creatures rather like nautiluses were probably the ancestors of other cephalopods. These included the ammonites or rams whose shells were often heavily ornamented with ribs or spines. Some ammonites had huge horn shells but they all became extinct 100 million years ago. Nobody knows why. The mystery of their extinction is just as great as the mystery surrounding the death of the dinosaurs. The nautiluses, which changed less over the centuries, have been the survivors.

▼ Below, you can see a group of cephalopods as you might have seen them swimming about in the sea 150 million years ago. The coiled creatures are ammonites. The largest ammonites had shells that were 6 feet across. The ammonites became extinct 100 million years ago.

The long, straight creatures are belemnites. Belemnites were similar to present-day squids. Like squids, they had hooked tentacles and ink sacs.

NEOPILINA

In 1952, some small creatures were found in deep water off the coast of Mexico. They looked like flattened limpets, but they turned out to be very different. Limpets have a single big muscle attaching their soft bodies to their shells. These "new" creatures had several blocks of muscles and pairs of gills. This is like a creature called *Pilina*, known only as a fossil from rocks over 500 million years old. The new find was named *Neopilina*, which means "new Pilina." *Neopilina* has not changed over time, but it has certainly altered its habitat. It is only found in deep water, unlike its fossil ancestors. In the deep sea, it has few enemies and this probably accounts for its survival.

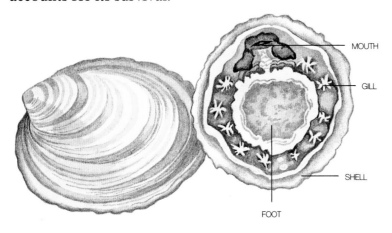

MOUTH

GILL

SHELL

FOOT

◄ On the left, you can see the top of *Neopilina's* shell and the underside of its body. There are five pairs of gills, with which the animal breathes, and a muscular foot that it uses to crawl across the ocean floor. *Neopilina* eats tiny creatures that it gathers from the ocean bottom.

Deep Sea Exploration
In submersibles, like the one shown here, scientists can watch life in the deep sea. More often they work in floating laboratories, such as the Danish marine research vessel *Galathea*, which dredged up the first specimens of *Neopilina*. Geologists, physicists, chemists, and marine biologists study the ocean floor, seawater, and marine plants and animals. This work helps us to understand an important part of our environment. *Neopilina* is not the only living fossil to have been discovered in the deep sea; others may be found in the future.

HORSESHOE CRABS

Horseshoe crabs are not true crabs. They are related to spiders and scorpions, though they do not have a poisonous bite or sting. Horseshoe crabs' bodies are divided into two main sections, both covered with a strong, leathery shell. The front part, which is horseshoe shaped, has insectlike **compound eyes** on its upper surface. The smaller, back part ends in a long spine.

Fossil horseshoe crabs are found in Silurian rocks as much as 430 million years old. Horseshoe crabs have changed very little since then. Today, five species survive, the largest of them about 16 inches long. They live in shallow water off the east coast of North America and in parts of the Indian and east Pacific oceans. They crawl over the ocean floor, hunting the worms and other small animals and plants on which they feed.

In some areas, humans scoop up **spawning** horseshoe crabs to use as **fertilizer** on the land. They are protected against most other enemies by their armor. If one is turned on its back, however, it is almost helpless. Only in soft sand can the crab use its long tail-spine to flip itself right-side up.

▶ Here, you can see a female horseshoe crab (bottom left) laying her eggs on a beach. Her eggs are being **fertilized** by three male crabs. The eggs will hatch into young that grow and change slowly. The young will shed their shells at least 12 times and do not become adult until they are about three years old.

▼ Below, you can see horseshoe crabs as they looked 400 million years ago. Horseshoe crabs have changed very little over time. One of the reasons they have survived may be that they have few natural enemies. Beneath the hard shell is a small body, which is not very nourishing food for a hunter.

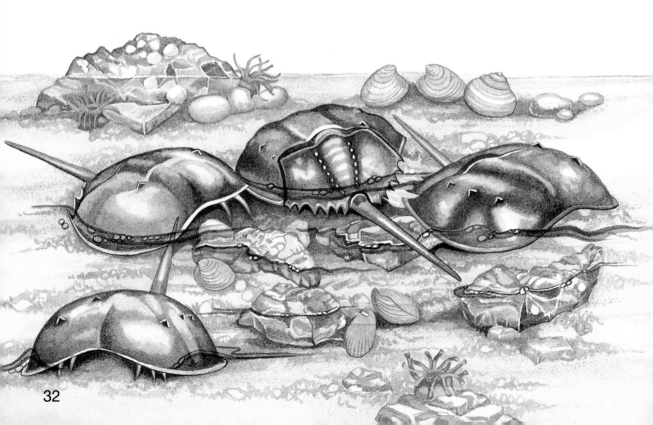

The Sea Scorpion

Horseshoe crabs have never been very big animals. The sea scorpions, which were their closest relatives, were the largest **arthropods** of all time. The giants among them were about 9 feet long. These monsters were most important during the Silurian Period, about 450 to 420 million years ago. Only the best-armored creatures survived attacks from their tremendous pincers and jaws. Some were powerful swimmers and others were burrowers, but both kinds became extinct about 240 million years ago. The slow, shuffling horseshoe crabs survived.

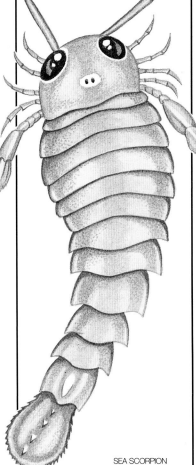

PINCERS

Large Shell, Little Body

If you turn a horseshoe crab over, you can see that its large shell covers a little body. At the head end is a pair of small pincers for seizing food. Behind these are four pairs of legs used for walking, followed by one pair used mainly for digging. The bases of the legs are thickened and spiny. They are used to chew food. This is not as odd as you might think, because the horseshoe crab's legs surround its mouth. On the hind part of the body are the oarlike gills. By flapping their gills hard, horseshoe crabs sometimes swim slowly, and clumsily.

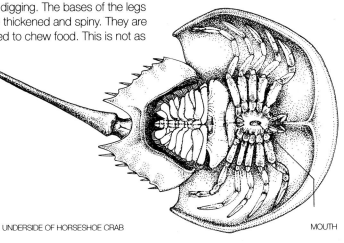

UNDERSIDE OF HORSESHOE CRAB   MOUTH

SEA SCORPION

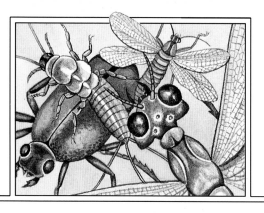

INSECTS

Insects are not very common as fossils because most of them are small and fragile land-dwellers. Their remains are destroyed before they can become fossilized. The remains that have been found, however, show that some insects have not changed for millions of years.

EARLY INSECTS

Plants first appeared on land 400 million years ago. As they did so, small creatures moved onto the land with them. Some of the earliest evidence of insects comes from Scotland. Here, some fossil plants that lived about 380 million years ago show signs of damage like that

▼ The first insects were probably like silverfish of today. So far, the earliest fossils of silverfish date back only about 40 million years, but the way they are formed is evidence of an earlier form of life. These creatures never have wings. As they grow, they molt a large number of times, even after they are able to mate and lay eggs.

PRESENT-DAY SILVERFISH

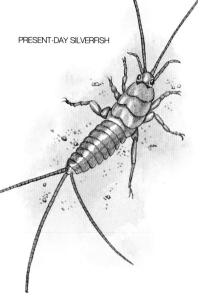

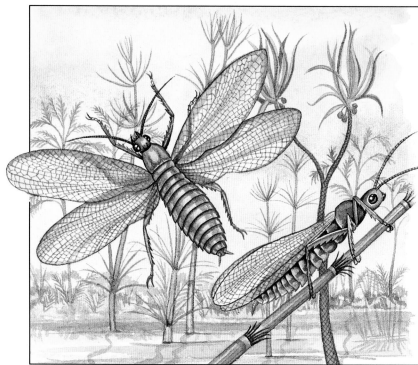

Fossil Grasshopper
This picture is of some early grasshopperlike creatures that lived about 350 million years ago. They were probably good runners, but they did not hop, for all of their legs were the same length. They also had large wings, so it is likely that they could fly well. They were quite large insects, up to about 4 inches in length. They would have made a good meal for amphibians on the ground, or for dragonflies in the air, so they needed their speed to escape. The first fossils of hopping and singing grasshoppers date back about 280 million years.

caused by present-day insects. Among the plants are fossils of springtails, which are thought to be the ancestors of all sorts of insects.

As time went on, insects became more varied. Some turned from being scavengers and plant eaters to becoming hunters. Some early insects were large. One dragonflylike species had a wingspan of 30 inches. When flowering plants **evolved**, insects, because of their ability to fly, found a new way of life as **pollinators**.

▲ This dragonfly lived in forests 280 million years ago. All dragonflies are hunters, feeding mainly on other flying insects. Unfortunately, the prey of extinct dragonflies were rarely preserved. But we know that they exist. The photograph shows a present-day dragonfly.

Some modern dragonflies are able to fold their wings over their backs, which the early kinds could not do. In spite of this, they still beat their wings individually. You can hear them clacking against each other as a dragonfly patrols the air looking for other insects to eat.

Wing Development

Insect wings first developed as three pairs of flaps growing from the upper side of the **thorax**. You can see how this looked in the picture of an early insect below. This insect probably flapped two wings on one side of its body as it flapped one wing on the other side. This was not very efficient and, in time, the front pair of wings disappeared. All present-day insects, like the lacewing shown below, have four wings at most.

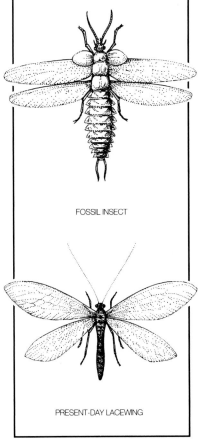

FOSSIL INSECT

PRESENT-DAY LACEWING

BEETLES

The earliest fossil beetles date back about 230 million years. They had tough forewings, but their structure shows that these were flapped in flight, rather than being used to give lift, as with modern beetles. During the Mesozoic Era, beetles were common. Most were scavengers, wood feeders, or hunters. Some turned to feeding on pollen. Fossils of cycad flowers with damage to the developing seeds have been found. Beetles were probably the cause of this. Flowering plants have enclosed **ovules**, which are less likely to be damaged by beetles.

▼ *Protorabus* is the first known ground beetle. Its remains, which date back about 135 million years, were found in Central Asia. Ground beetles became common in the latter part of the Mesozoic Era. They were hunters and probably fed on other insects and grubs, just as their descendants do today. *Carabus violaceus* is a modern ground beetle.

PROTORABUS

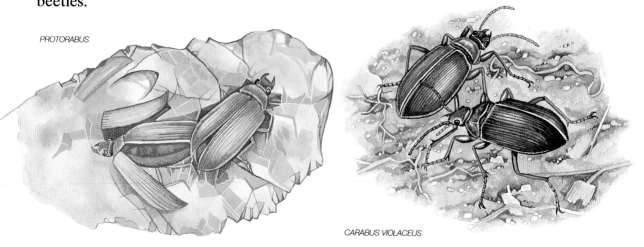

CARABUS VIOLACEUS

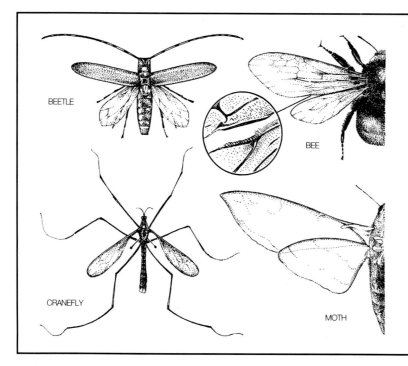

BEETLE

BEE

CRANEFLY

MOTH

More Advanced Wings

Most good insect fliers use their two pairs of wings as a single unit on each side of the body. Butterflies and moths hook and overlap the forewings and hind wings, so they are forced to beat together. Bees and wasps have a series of small hooks that link the two pairs of wings. Beetles, which use their hardened forewings to protect their bodies when they are on the ground, hold them up in the air to gain lift, but only flap the hind wings. Flies beat only their forewings; the hind ones have become very small and are used as balancers. This is one of the reasons that some flies can hover, somersault, and even fly backward!

BEES AND BUTTERFLIES

Butterflies and bees both depend on **nectar** for their food. Their ancestors may have lived at the same time as the dinosaurs, but they left no identifiable remains. Wood-boring and gall-making relatives of bees lived in Mesozoic forests. True bees and wasps, however, are known only from periods nearer to the present day. We find their fossils dating back 60 million years, when the nectar-bearing flowering plants became more common. Butterfly fossils are very similar to living species.

▼ Below, you can see a fossil swallowtail butterfly next to a present-day relative. Insect eaters often eat the soft bodies of butterflies and moths. The broad, hard wings are not often eaten and sometimes become fossilized. Often they are well-preserved, and in fine-grained mudstones they sometimes show color patterns. We can only guess what color this fossil swallowtail was, but it was probably black and yellow, like many swallowtails.

FOSSIL BUTTERFLY

PRESENT-DAY SWALLOWTAIL BUTTERFLY

Insect in Amber
The picture on the left is of a long-legged fly preserved in amber. Amber is formed from fossilized tree gum. As it flows from slight wounds in the trunk, it often traps small animals. These include many small and fragile insects. It is impossible to know what the insides of an insect in amber look like. However, details of the finest scales or hairs on the surface are preserved. Amber from the Baltic region of Europe contains many insects.

PLANTS

Life on earth depends on water. This is specially so at the beginning of each new generation of plants and animals. In the most ancient types of plants, the life of a new plant starts with a male cell that swims through water to fertilize a female cell.

FERNS AND HORSETAILS

Plants without flowers include mosses, ferns, and horsetails. These can all be described as living fossils, because there are many fossils known of all of them. Water plays an important part in making a new generation in these plants.

Invasion of the land by plants probably began about 400 million years ago. They lived in swampy places, where there was plenty of water. As time went on, they developed stiffer, woody stems. This meant that they were able to stretch up toward the light and that they needed to carry water from the roots to where it was used. Leaves first appeared as outgrowths from the stems. Differences developed in ways of growth, leaf form, and spores, giving rise to new kinds of plants. Some early plants that were important parts of their environment were club mosses, horsetails, and ferns.

▼ About 300 million years ago great forests covered much of the **lowlands** of the northern world. Their remains formed coal.

The coal forests were green like today's woodlands. There were few other colors, for none of the plants had flowers, though perhaps the pollenlike **spores** that sifted through the leaves were golden or orange. The trees that formed these forests would look unfamiliar today. The cushioned bark of the scale trees and the whorled leaves of the giant horsetails were unlike any living trees. The groups of plants to which they belonged have survived, although their modern descendants seem shrunken and unimportant in the modern world of flowering plants.

Ancient Giants, Modern Dwarves

Some kinds of nonflowering plants that are now quite small were once giants. Today's club mosses are usually found in warm, damp forests. Their creeping, leafy stems rarely rise more than 10 inches above the ground. In the damp forests of the Carboniferous Period, 300 million years ago, they formed great trees, known as scale trees. These trees were almost 100 feet tall.

The biggest horsetails of today are less than 6 feet high. In the forests of the past they grew to be about 30 feet tall. Some ferns in early forests were climbers, like present-day ivy. Others became treelike, growing to a height of 30 feet. In the tropics of today, some tree ferns survive but most are smaller than this.

SCALE TREE

PRESENT-DAY CLUB MOSS

CYCADS AND GINGKOS

The cycads and the gingko tree must have been the food of some of the leaf-chewing dinosaurs. These living fossils are a link between the first, spore-producing plants and the seed plants of today. They have almost solved the problem of being dependent on water during the breeding season.

The early nonflowering plants lived in water, and a male cell swam to the female so that fertilization could take place. On land, plants, not being able to move about created a breeding problem, which was overcome when early plants lived in damp places and produced a male cell that could swim to the female part of the plant. Eventually, the male cell became a waxy-coated spore, which could be carried by the wind.

The cycads and the gingko have male spores of this kind. The female parts of the plant lie inside a woody stone. Above them is a drop of liquid. The spore releases a male cell that swims through the liquid by beating tiny hairs until it reaches the female cell. The distance that the males have to travel is tiny, but the journey takes months. True conifers and flowering plants do not need water for fertilization to take place.

▶ Here, you can see the fruits of the gingko tree. Gingkos are found in the wild in one tiny area of China, but for many centuries they were taken from there and grown in temple courtyards. Gingkos were first seen by Europeans in 1690 and brought to Europe soon after. Now they are often used as ornamental trees in gardens and parks. Usually male trees are grown, because the fruits produced by the females smell bad when they start to decay. In spite of this they are used as food in parts of China.

▼ Cycads are found today in the tropics, often in dry or rugged places. Gigantic female **cones**, which may weigh almost 20 pounds each, snuggle in the middle of a tuft of palmlike leaves at the top of a stumpy trunk. The whole time scale of a cycad's life is a slow one. A cycad may live for over 1,000 years. Growth is slow; even the process of fertilization of the egg takes months.

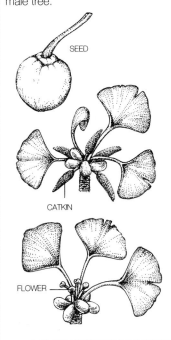

Separate Sexes
Each gingko tree is either male or female. The female flowers grow from a short woody lump on the twigs. Male catkins grow in clusters from similar lumps on the male tree.

SEED

CATKIN

FLOWER

▼ For much of the last 60 million years, woodlands covered most of the northern world, even in what is now the cold lands of the tundra.

A general cooling of the climate since the days of the dinosaurs has reduced the places where trees live. This map shows where forests can

grow today, though in many areas they have been cut down. In spite of this, a few ancient plants survive from earlier, warmer times.

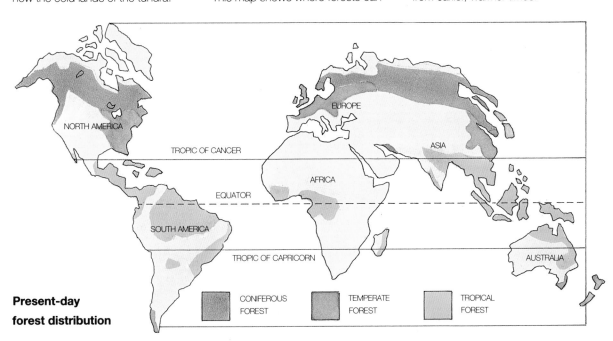

EUROPE

NORTH AMERICA

TROPIC OF CANCER

ASIA

AFRICA

EQUATOR

SOUTH AMERICA

TROPIC OF CAPRICORN

AUSTRALIA

CONIFEROUS FOREST

TEMPERATE FOREST

TROPICAL FOREST

Present-day forest distribution

MAGNOLIAS

A time traveler, going back to the end of the age of dinosaurs would find the world had a familiar look. The main reason for this is that by then flowering plants had taken over from the less colorful cycads and gingkos. Many of the early flowering plants are now extinct, but some groups still survive. The magnolia family is among them. Magnolias are mostly large-leaved forest trees and shrubs that can be found in many parts of North America and Asia. They have leaflike petals and fruit that look a bit like a cone.

◀ Tulip trees, like the one shown here, are members of the magnolia family. They can grow to a height of 200 feet.

▼ Magnolia flowers, like these, are often seen growing in gardens. They have been taken all over the world, far from the places where they survive as living fossils.

Early tarsiers (pages 20-22) may have scrambled among the branches of trees like this 50 million years ago searching for the beetles that pollinated the flowers.

MAGNOLIA FLOWERS

THE DAWN REDWOOD

Like magnolias, dawn redwoods first developed at the end of the Mesozoic Era. At that time they grew in much the same area as the tulip trees, but about 15 million years ago they became extinct in North America and Europe. As a fossil, it was not recognized until 1941. Then, scientists who were studying extinct trees, decided that some specimens that they had were not redwoods as they had first thought. They called the newly-recognized fossil *Metasequoia*, or dawn redwood. Only six years later it was found living in a remote part of China.

▼ Until 1941, only fossils of the dawn redwood, like the one shown below, were known. When living dawn redwoods were first discovered in Hupey Province in southeast China, less than 1,000 trees survived in the wild. Fortunately, dawn redwoods could be grown easily in parks and gardens and in 1948 seed was exported to the United States. From there seed was passed around the world. Today, dawn redwoods are often seen in areas where they have been extinct for 20 million years.

Unlike most other conifers, dawn redwoods are **deciduous**. They turn a beautiful golden color and shed their leaves in the fall.

DAWN REDWOOD FOSSIL

INTO THE FUTURE

We humans are the one great enemy now bringing extinction nearer for many living fossils. We explore remote places and often take diseases and destruction to the plants and animals that live there. Many remote island animals have died out because of this. We cut down forests and often cause large-scale pollution, hugely damaging to ourselves as well as other creatures. Often we cause problems by our curiosity. It is likely that coelacanths are nearer to total extinction now than at any time during the last 80 million years. This is because we have been killing them so that we can find out more about them.

Although we humans are so destructive, we can also be helpful. We know what the problems are. If we put our talents towards conservation, the future may not be so bleak as it sometimes seems. With our help, the living fossils may stay that way, and not become real fossils in the near future.

Why Have They Survived?
A few types of living fossils such as horseshoe crabs and sharks may have survived through great spans of time because no other creatures have been more successful at what they do.

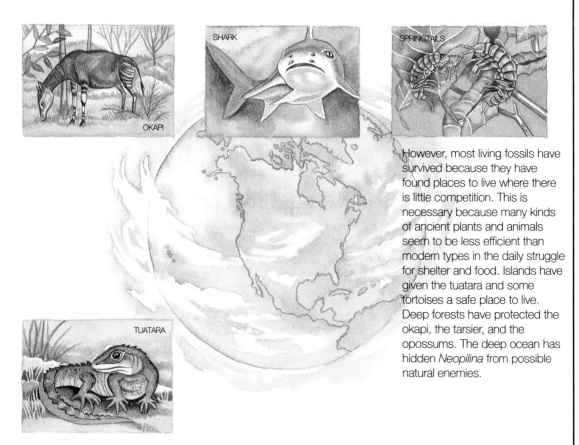

OKAPI

SHARK

SPRINGTAILS

TUATARA

However, most living fossils have survived because they have found places to live where there is little competition. This is necessary because many kinds of ancient plants and animals seem to be less efficient than modern types in the daily struggle for shelter and food. Islands have given the tuatara and some tortoises a safe place to live. Deep forests have protected the okapi, the tarsier, and the opossums. The deep ocean has hidden *Neopilina* from possible natural enemies.

GLOSSARY

ARTHROPOD An animal with a hard outer skeleton made of hornlike material called chitin. Its legs and feet are jointed. There are more arthropods than any other sorts of animals. Insects, spiders, and crabs are all arthropods.

CARAPACE The upper part of the shell of a tortoise or crab.

CARTILAGE A gristly material that forms part of the skeleton of sharks and is replaced by bone in most other vertebrates.

COMPOUND EYES The eyes of some arthropods in which each eye has many separate lenses. Eyes of this kind are very good at detecting movement.

CONE The part of some plants that carries spores or seeds in a leaflike or woody structure and arranged around a central stem.

CONSERVATION The protection of animals, plants, and habitats.

DECIDUOUS Plants that shed all of their leaves at a particular time, for example, in the fall.

ENDANGERED The status of increasing numbers of plants and animals which, largely due to human activity, are so rare that they are nearly extinct.

ENVIRONMENT The overall surroundings in which an animal or plant lives.

EVOLVE To develop changes in plants or animals that occur over time.

EXTINCT Species that no longer exist.

FERTILIZE To bring together male and female sex cells, of plants or animals, so that a new generation is formed.

FERTILIZER Minerals in water or soil that help plants grow.

FILTER FEEDER A water-living animal that feeds on small organisms that it strains from its surroundings, often using a mesh of fine gills.

HABITAT The natural home of a plant or animal. The word often implies a wide area, such as a forest or a seashore.

LENS A transparent structure in eyes. Light passes through the lens to a sensitive area where the image of what the animal sees is formed.

LOPHOPHORE A structure inside the body of a brachiopod (lamp shell).

LOWLANDS Low-lying parts of the earth's surface.

NECTAR A sugary substance produced by flowers to attract pollinators.

NOCTURNAL Active at night.

OPPOSABLE A thumb or big toe that can be folded across the palm of the hand or the sole of the foot.

OVULE The female part of a plant that develops into a seed after fertilization.

PALEONTOLOGIST A person who studies fossils.

PLASTRON The lower part of the shell of a tortoise or turtle.

POLLINATE To carry the male cells of a flower (the pollen) to the female parts where fertilization takes place.

POUCH An outside pocket. Some mammals produce very tiny young that are then protected in a pouch.

PREDATOR A hunter.

PREHENSILE TAIL A tail that is flexible and strong enough to hold things.

PREY The animals caught and eaten by predators.

REPTILE An air-breathing vertebrate animal, with a hard, dry skin, often armored with scales or bone. Reptiles are cold-blooded and their young usually hatch from eggs, though a few kinds give birth to living babies.

RODENT A mammal with two strong front teeth in its upper and lower jaws, which it uses for gnawing. Squirrels, mice, and porcupines are all rodents.

SEPTUM A partition between two areas, for example, the bone that separates the nostrils.

SIPHUNCLE The porous tube that runs through the chambers of the shell of a nautilus or ammonite.

SNOUT The part of an animal's head that lies in front of its braincase.

SPAWN The eggs of fishes or amphibians, or the act of producing them.

SPECIES A kind of animal or plant distinct from all other kinds. In nature, members of a species are capable of mating and producing normal young. Members of different species are rarely able to mate with each other. If they do, the young often do not survive.

SPORES Very small parts of plants, which become detached from the parent plant and are involved in forming a new generation.

THORAX The chest part of an animal. In insects the area where the legs and wings are attached.

VERTEBRATE An animal with a backbone.

INDEX

Illustrations are indicated in **bold**

A TEMPLAR BOOK

Devised and produced by The Templar Company plc
Pippbrook Mill, London Road, Dorking, Surrey RH4 1JE
Copyright © 1991 by The Templar Company plc

PHOTOGRAPHIC CREDITS
t = top, b = bottom, l = left, r = right
All photographs supplied by Bruce Coleman Ltd
Front cover Jane Burton
Back cover Leonard Lee Rue III
Page 7 Frances Furlong; *page 9* Michel Viard; *page 11* Norman Tomalin;
page 15 l Bill Wood, *r* Leonard Lee Rue III; *page 17* Frances Furlong;
page 19 Leonard Lee Rue III; *page 21* John Mackinnon; *page 23* Joseph van
Wormer; *page 25* Francisco Futil; *page 26* John Cancalosi; *page 29* William E.
Townsend Jr; *page 31* Jeff Simon; *page 33* Leonard Lee Rue III; *page 35*
Dr Frieder Sauer; *page 37* Gunter Ziesler; *page 41* Hans Reinhard;
page 42 Eric Chrichton; *page 43* Michel Viard.